Always forgive your enemies:
nothing annoys them so much.

the quotations of

OSCAR WILDE

the drawings of

SIMON DREW

Religion is the fashionable substitute for belief

ANTIQUE COLLECTORS' CLUB

to Caroline

The Alps are objects of
appallingly bad taste.

©2004 Simon Drew
World copyright reserved

ISBN 1 85149 477 4

British Library Cataloguing-in-Publication Data
A catalogue record for this book is available from the British Library

Printed in England
by the Antique Collectors' Club Ltd., Woodbridge, Suffolk

It is always a silly thing
to give advice, but to
give good advice is fatal.

Oscar Wilde

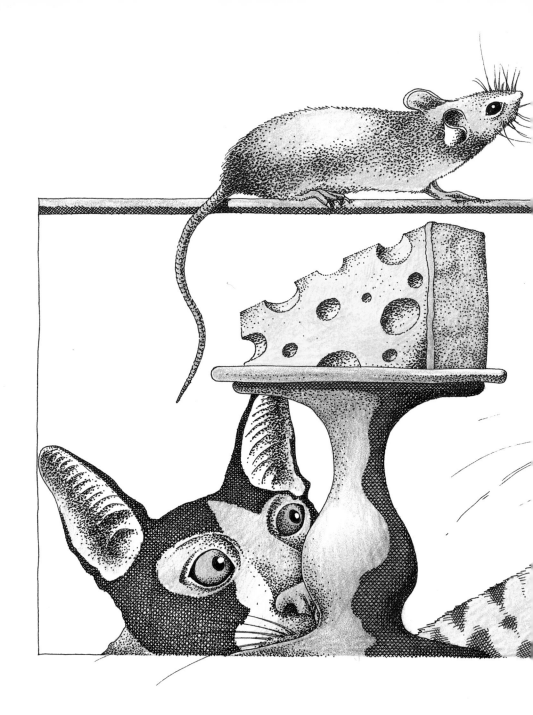

4

she who hesitates is won

After a good dinner
one can forgive anybody,
even one's own
relations.   Oscar Wilde

A gentleman never insults
someone unintentionally.

One should either be a work of art,
or wear a work of art.

There is only one thing
worse than being talked
about, and that is not
being talked about.
Oscar Wilde

Few parents nowadays pay any regard to what their children say to them. The old fashioned respect for the young is fast dying out.

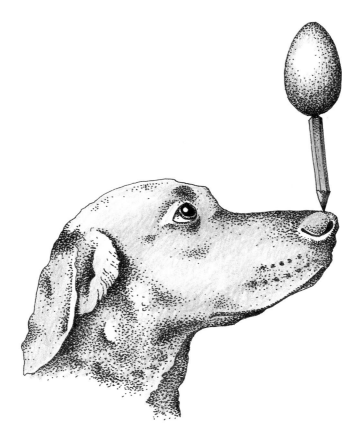

Experience is the name
everyone gives
to their mistakes.

Oscar Wilde

No gentleman ever has any money and no gentleman ever takes exercise.

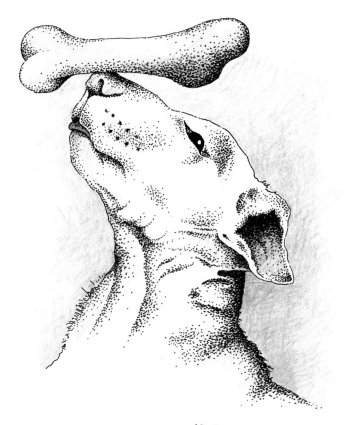

There are terrible
temptations that it requires
strength and courage to
yield to.   Oscar Wilde

Fashion is a form of ugliness
so intolerable that we have to
alter it every six months.

Looking good and dressing well
are essential:
a purpose in life is not.

Duty is what one
expects from others.
It is not what one does
oneself.   Oscar Wilde

It is most dangerous for a husband to pay any attention to his wife in public. It always makes people think that he beats her when they are alone.

Women love men for
their defects; if men have
enough of them women will
forgive them everything.
Oscar Wilde

To win back my youth, there is nothing I wouldn't do — except take exercise, get up early or be a useful member of the community.

A cheque is
the only argument
I understand.
Oscar Wilde

I never travel without my diary. One should always have something sensational to read in the train.

23

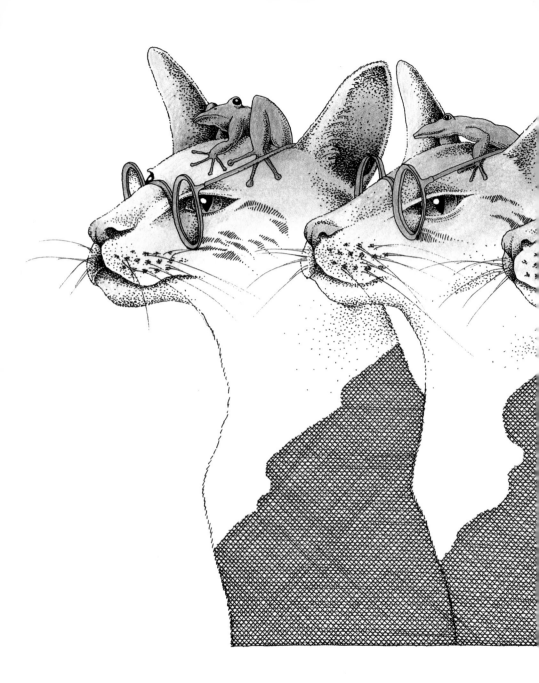

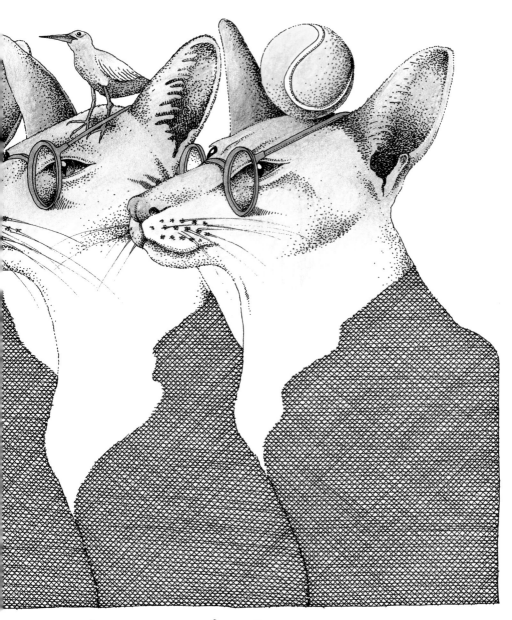

seriousness is the
only refuge of the shallow

Young people imagine
that money is everything
and when they get
older they know it is.
Oscar Wilde

I don't want money.
It's only people who
pay their bills
who want money.

Oscar Wilde

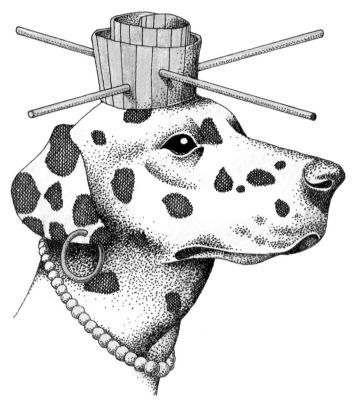

Thirty-five is a
very attractive age.
London society is full of
women who have, of their
own free choice, remained
thirty-five for years.
Oscar Wilde

When people agree
with me, I always feel
that I must be wrong.

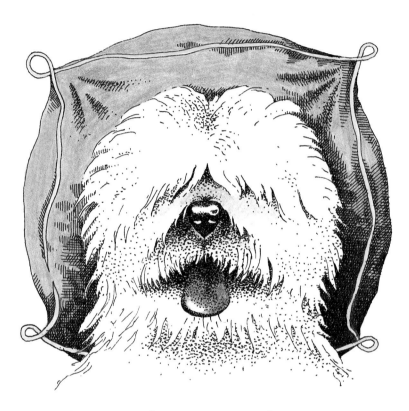

Work is the refuge
of people who
have nothing
better to do.
                    Oscar Wilde

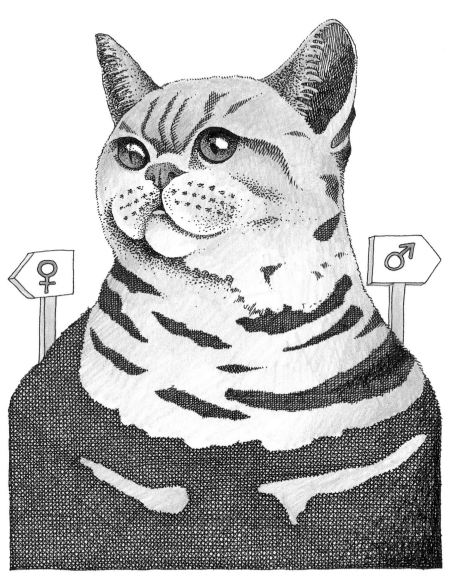

I like men who have a future
and women who have a past.

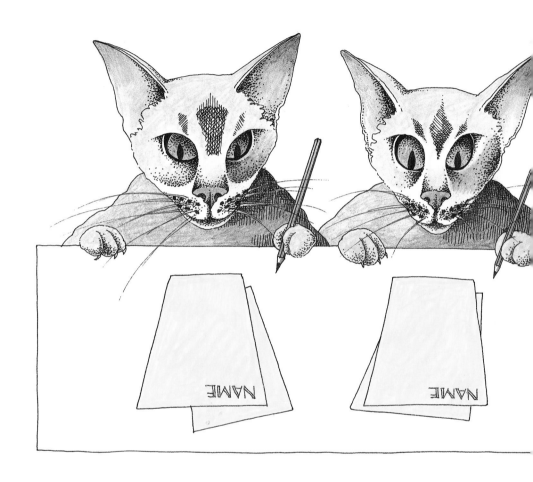

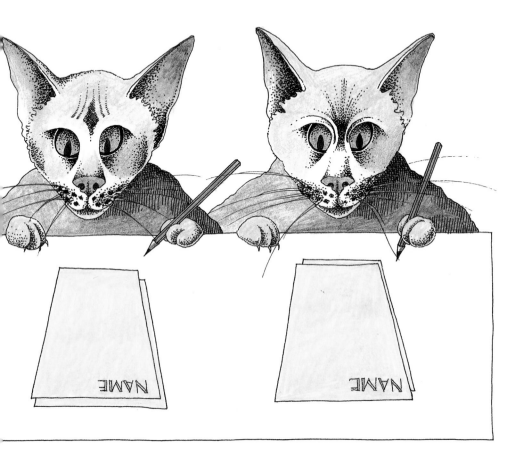

In examinations the foolish ask
questions that the wise cannot
answer.

Life is one fool thing
after another.
Whereas love is
two fool things
after each other.

Oscar Wilde

The Book of Life begins with
a man and a woman in a
garden.
  It ends with Revelations.

Women have a much
better time than men in this
world. There are far more
things forbidden to them.
Oscar Wilde

No crime is vulgar
but
all vulgarity is crime.

The truth is
rarely pure,
and never simple.

Oscar Wilde

Only dull people are
bright at breakfast.

The first duty in life is to be
as artificial as possible.

Rich bachelors should be
heavily taxed. It's not fair
that some men should be
happier than others.
Oscar Wilde

I can't help detesting
my relations. I suppose
it comes from the fact
that none of us can
stand other people having
the same faults as ourselves.

Of course, America had
often been discovered
before Columbus, but
it had always been
hushed up. Oscar Wilde

The old believe everything:
the middle-aged suspect
everything: the young
know everything.

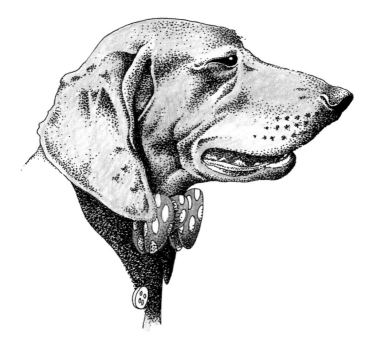

Fashion is what one
wears oneself.

Oscar Wilde

If one tells the truth
one is sure,
sooner or late,
to be found out.

Anyone who lives within their means suffers from a lack of imagination. Oscar Wilde

I have to choose between
this world, the next
and Australia.